Other books by Mark Allen Gray ...

Rocking in a Free World

Embedded in America

and other works under construction.

I0158707

Gray Technologies Press

The
Hounds of Love

The Hounds of Love

by
Mark Allen Gray

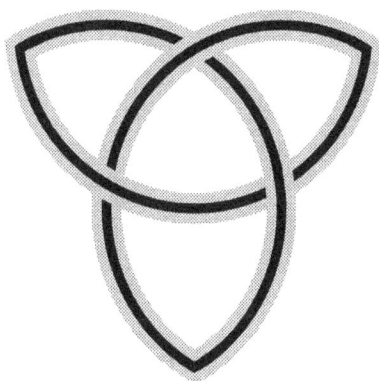

Gray Technologies Press

The Hounds of Love

Published 2004 by
Gray Technologies Press
502 Hanna Road
Bel Air, Maryland, 21014 United States of America
www.graytechpress.com

Library of Congress Control Number: 2004111551

ISBN 0-9761095-1-4

Printed in the United States of America.

Revision Number 2004.09.29.01

Gray Technologies Press

Dedication

This book is dedicated to my family in appreciation for all of their love and support. The strength of a family's love will surely keep the hounds at bay.

Contents

Introduction

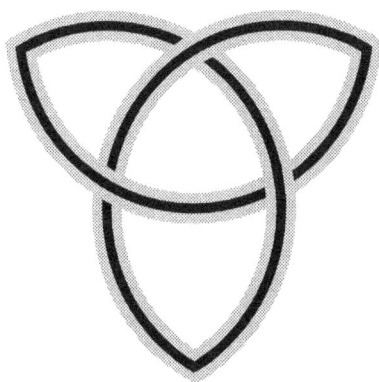

The Hounds of Love is a collection of poems that spans a period of 27 years of writing and 43 years of life. After a near-fatal car accident, the author was compelled to assemble and share these poems in a story. Each poem looks at love in a different emotional light. There is no deep hidden meaning in this story nor are there any solutions to love's troubles, only an echo of the profound affect of love on humanity. The poems simply and collectively tell a familiar story in an unrestrained free verse form through the personal experience and voice of the author.

This is the story of love discovered, love lived, love lost, and love rediscovered. Probably the reader has experienced some or all of these. If this is the case, then the reader will know that love has no form, no rules, and no boundaries. It is free and it is loose and it is dogged by all of us, relentlessly. Like a pack of hounds on a hunt, it is a game, with one prize, and one loser.

Individually, each poem is a distillation of an intense emotional event. The thread that binds them is free will and the results of choices made, for better or for worse. We all make choices and we all must deal with the consequences.

Every story, of course, should have a point, as a point in all directions is no point at all. The point of this story is that love is a fundamental and necessary component of the human condition. In the process of discovering and embracing love, we find that love has a life and a cycle of its own, independent of our plans, our hopes, and our dreams. Love challenges each of us and in doing so, our strengths and our weakness become self evident. By confronting and conquering love's challenges, we grow as humans.

In this story there are three main characters: the narrator, My Love, and My Friend. Since this is a collection of poetry on a theme, the characters do not develop in the traditional sense typical of prose. Character development in this story is rooted square on the narrator, and the narrator interacts with the other characters through a series of four chapters: Discovery, Experience, Loss, and Resolve. These four phases collectively form a life cycle. Cycles, of course, repeat.

The story begins with the harsh reality of being born into this world. This begins the phase of discovery. From birth through childhood, adolescence, and adulthood there is a continuous stream of discovery. In fact, it never ends. There is the discovery of different types of love, the discovery of sex, the discovery of romance and loneliness, and the discovery of love in art and literature.

With discovery follows experience, experience of all that love has and does not have to offer. Love is a game and games have strategy and there are victors and there are losers. There are good moves and there are bad moves, but moves are made and we move on. There is the search for "the one" and there is the problem of men and women just being friends. Can they be?

With experience and victory also comes loss. Play the game long enough and you will lose a match. Loss of love, whatever type of love, family, friend, or lover, is a deeply painful experience. Emptiness, despair, fear, anger, hatred, and self-commiseration are found in the wells of loss. It is very difficult to climb back out, to restore your self and your life.

To conquer loss there is resolve. Resolve requires the element of logic and the strength of will. Resolve requires us to pull ourselves out of our hole and to remember those that love us and to embrace their love and to let them help us. And for those that believe in a higher power, we must not forsake our faith.

Thus resolve ends the cycle of discovery, experience, and loss. This cycle unfortunately is repeatable by definition, but having gone through the cycle once, we should be wiser and more resolved the next time around.

Each chapter in this story begins with a graphic symbol. These symbols are a creation of the author. They bear a resemblance to Celtic symbols, but vary in detail and meaning. Each ring contains three circles representing birth, life, and death. Chapter One is represented by the first ring, the ring of Love Discovered. The second chapter adds a second ring, the ring of Love Experienced. The third chapter adds a third ring, the ring of Love Lost. The fourth and final chapter resolves the three rings into a single interlocking symbol in the shape of a heart. The heart symbol suggests that love is an endless cycle of discovery, experience, and loss. It is a tragic realization that love is never fully experienced without discovery and loss.

Though love has no form and no boundaries, the use of the ring symbology is intended to put an infinite concept into finite tangible terms, giving love form and boundaries that we can visualize, grasp, and hold on to. Resolving love into a heart shape is a universally accepted symbol.

Love is a big subject to explore. Writers and artists of all types have been driven by its mystery, thrill, and madness for many millennia. It is the author's hope that the reader will find some entertainment or healing value in this small story.

"Every man who does not accept the conditions of life sells his soul, for he is trying to escape from human liberty and its indispensable suffering."

— Charles Baudelaire

Chapter One:
Discovery

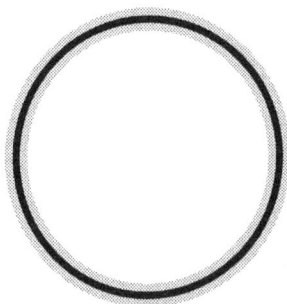

Peering Through Hungry Eyes

Birth gives us sex,
That builds our walls.

Life creates a void,
To fill with fear.

Death unsexes,
And gives us wings,
Where once we had claws.

Forces

What is it that connects people?

Is it gravity, chemistry, psychology, or
something more?

We are each born alone and disconnected from
the whole.

A loose spirit instanced to a few pounds of
bone and flesh.

A new house on a new ride through this space
and this time.

Why?
Do we have purpose?
Does destiny exist only in a dream?
Should God call upon me, will I be ready?
Is he here?

There are forces at work,
Beyond your imagination,
Primal and complex, at once.

Rocket Man

Summer dreams
Mildewy cotton canvas tent palaces
Trees our big brothers
Building handy work nest forts
To vacation gods, we worshiped
In boyish realization
Of feminine mystique

Deep mysteries
To wonder and fathom
Testing ourselves
Pushing the buttons
In this 20th century dreamscape
Merlyn in a tin can
Rocket man

Lost Boys

Sneaky deceptions
Parental discretions
Failing in favor of sex talk
In fields of new freedom
New responsibility

There is a greatness
In the retrospective light
That shines on being free

The boy becomes a man
In a single thought
Carnal knowledge

Fresh Air

I breathed deeply and sighed
If only we could have touched
In that far out reaching sense
That progresses in the way
When you are a child
And all the world
Is so simple
And clean
And bold
And bright
And full of the great lightness
Of being

Where is the Love

Where is the love?

Is it in a mother
When she looks on the face
Of her sleeping son?

Is it in a man
When he holds her hand
And understands?

Is it in the boy
When he says out of the blue,
"I love you Mom and Dad"?

Is it in the man on the cross
When he asks his God
"Please forgive them"?

Humanity has spent centuries
Trying to define love
But there is no question
That we can find love
Wherever we find humanity

I am both sad and glad
To be human
My cats are gentle soft ebony
Do they have an opinion
Of their felinity?

The Sea of Love

Picture this
A ship on a great sea
A soul adrift on a dark
And windy day
The sails down
A light beams
From beneath the deck
The waves rising
In relentless progression

Lightning strikes
Into the abyss
Shadows form
In an instant
On the deck
On the sea
Then lost
Boom! Boom! Crash!
Did you forget?

Thunder rumbles
All around
The waves swelling
And pushing
Cresting and crashing
On the deck
The light below
Dry and bright, rides on
A photo for your album

Mysterious Union

Sun rise and sun set

Irony and pity

Bret and Jake

Slut and clown

Mysterious union

Consider the Love

Consider the love

Of Romeo and Juliet
Young, swift, and tragic

Of Brett and Jake
Old, slow, and comic

Of Shakespeare and Hemingway
Eternal, steady, and complete

Mentors of love's tragic and comic forms
For our entertainment, and our tears

Consider the love
It may serve you well

The Perfect Union

Love and sex

They are without a doubt, mutually exclusive.
But, and there is always one to consider,
Are they really?

Love is bigger than sex
Love is sex-less and big and gender-less

Love is in your soul
Sex is in your cells

Love is in a smile
A hug, and a deed

Sex is in a thought
A realization, a choice

Love cannot be chosen
Love is bigger than us
Love chooses us
Love is divine
Sex is fun
Sex with love
Is perfect union

What Women Want

I've been looking at this movie title,
Sitting on my shelf for weeks,
What Women Want,
And I've been thinking of the answer.

The answer is that there is no answer.
Every woman is completely unique,
Like a snowflake,
Each unique.

Each can be beautiful and cold as ice,
At the same time.
Yet melt in your hand,
And quench a thirst,
And warm a heart.

Of Gold and Flesh

Women are gold in flesh
Measured inversely proportional
To the carat, in weight
Desired directly proportional
To the shape

Pure gold, soft and malleable
Like the virgin woman child
On the bed
No
Not tonight

No thing has value
Without lust
Desire to have, fear of loss
A transaction of values
Of gold and of flesh

Loneliness

Sometimes I sit on the edge alone
And look at my world
Constructed from the pieces of love
That I have conquered and cached

When I'm alone, I fall to pieces
When I'm with you, I'm whole again
When I'm on the edge, I have visions
When I'm with you, I see again

On the edge are images of a future
That's not complete without you
Without My Love, I fall to pieces
Without my self, My Love is lost

Alone in the desert I took a ride
Lost myself, broke down and cried
Cried for my Father
Cried for my self
Cried for learning
Of the loneliness we're dealt

Chapter Two:
Experience

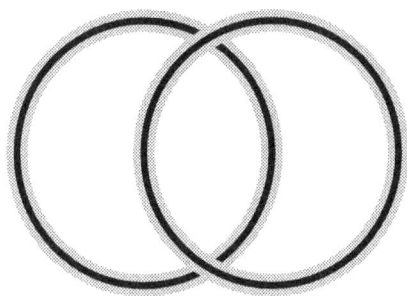

Single Victor

We've all been there
Even before the line began
A single victor enters the egg
The first game

So let the games begin!

Great Olympian feats
Thrills
Competition in the face of the void
Accomplishments

Trophies for your shelf

My Best Friend's Girl Friend

Once upon a time,
In a little town in New Mexico,
Far far away,
My best friend met this girl,
And it changed our lives.

She was good and she was bad,
She was everything but Mrs. Saad.
He was happy and he was glad,
He was always happy Mr. Saad.

The times, they were good,
The times, they were bad,
The times, they were everything,
And nothing we had.

But this girl, this woman,
He had met and held fast,
Was always a bright light,
In our dark happy mad.
Mad as a fiddle was I in his quest,
Of this lovely Spanish maiden,
A beautiful soul, no less.

So I drowned my loneliness,
In loud rock and roll,
And dreamed of meeting my mate,
My own soul-a-go-go.
And it happened at length,
That I met my girl too,

And then in a flash,
There were two happy dudes.

The times, they were good,
The times, they were bad,
The times, they were everything,
And nothing we had.

The Flower vs. The Tree

Dear Love,

Have you considered this?

Idealism, lost youth, confusion
Searching for answers
For teachers and friends

I'm like that sometimes,
But I take my medicine,
Temper my confusion,
By facing my problems
And dealing with them
In the real world.

Sure shit makes a beautiful flower
Grow in the springtime,
But it dies, when the summer heat,
Comes along.
Look! That's the same tree,
We saw last year!

But where have all of the flowers gone...

I love flowers, but give me trees!
Listen to him talk,
He's a shit-sucking flower,
Food for the trees.

Give me trees.

Strategy

You let him make the decisions,
You see everything through his mind set,
But what about yours?

Keep your vision, your mind-set.
Let him look through your eyes,
And see what a drag he really is.

Pain Relief

These words are real
Conversation is good
But it's transient
Like a pill
It wears off

We need a cure here,
Not another pain reliever.

Soul Food

Last week your hug gave me wings,
And I soared.

Today you bit my heart,
And I bleed.

The pain intoxicates,
Love feeds me.

Angles and vampires feast,
Food for the soul.

Are You Ready

I'm ready
The world is big
Please stay with me
In these dancing days
The woman knows the way
Time to play

It's crazy
These ways, these days
It's all in the heart
Howdy honey
I'll pay the dowry
I'm on salary

Her name was Love.
She was the morning sunshine through the
window on a spring day, warm and fun in the
way a summer run through the street excites
the boy child in boredom.

The bedroom was empty.
Her world was full.
An exchange perhaps, or a chemical reaction,
satisfaction.

Missed

Are those that I miss,
Those that miss me?
Are those that miss me,
Those that I miss?

The young are caught up in their lives
They forget about those
That have prepared their future
For better or for worse.

Grandfather is dying
30 minutes away
And I do not miss him, but I love him.
I wonder if he misses me.

She is lying
Next to me
And I miss her.
I wonder if she misses me.

Victory
Cannot be built
On misses.

Give Her a Kiss

The world is truly amazing to experience
Imagine if you had never been born
You would never have read these words
Or considered your own existence

You would have been nothing
And I would have been something
But I am nothing now
And you are something
To sit there and read this nonsense

Don't you have anything better to do?
Give her a kiss!

Bahama Blues

Two and two is four
Four and four is eight
Baby ain't this great
Back to the Bahamas
Sweet beach Taino

Eight is four
And four is two
Baby I've got you
Ramblin' on my mind
Sweet, sweet water beach and sky

When you've got a good friend
Treat her right
I can't see no reason why
The friend is woman, and the woman is wife

When you've got a good friend
Treat him right
I can't see no reason why
The friend is boy, and the boy is mine

When you've got a good son
Treat him right
I can't see no reason why
The boy is man and man must die

I really love that woman
Wonder why we can't agree
I really love that woman

She's always standin' by me

You better come home to my kitchen
Cause' it's gonna' be rainin'
A storm's a' brewin'

I went down to the crossroad
Got down on my knees
Jesus prayin' and big harmony

Thinkin' 'Bout My Woman

I woke up this mornin' baby

All my sperms were dead and gone

Was thinkin' 'bout you woman

The way you makes me weeps and moan

An Old Question

Can a man and a woman
Just be friends?
When Harry met Sally
Did you get the end?

For me now
It's only the start,
A study in time
And a place in my heart.

Should Have Known

It's in the way that she moves
Where was the last time
That she was in the room
Just because...

It's in the way that she smiles
When we first met
That was a long time ago
I really should have known

To Build a Fire

A smile
A touch
A thought
A connection
A filter
A transformation
A hug
An emotion
Play with fire
You will get burned

A Numb Surprise

There is no easy way out
Take a car and roll it
And wrap it
Around a telephone pole

Then drop back to Earth
At the push of a button
The seat belt
No easy way out

Shake the glass from your eyes
Feel the cold steel
Snapped tight
Around your wrists

Then sit in the back
And take a ride
A numb surprise

Black Snake

She's a crawling black snake
Crawling 'round our streets
Don't let her mess with your mate
Gonna' lose him
My Friend

She's a crawling black snake
Crawling through your door
If she looks you in the eye
Gonna' freeze you
My Friend

She's a crawling black snake
Crawling 'round your home
Don't let her watch your children
Gonna' make them bait
My Friend

She's a crawling black snake
Watch her shed her skin

Quiet Storm

There are those moments
Before a storm
A strange quality about the light
A sense of dusk before its time

Like a great still sea
Humbled by the tide
Like a Trojan horse
Waiting...

As the gods contemplate the next move
And the mortals cower
As the first low rumbles
Sound in the distance
And a breeze stirs
With warning
Of great troubles ahead

This is one of those moments.

Now I fear
For My Self
For My Love
For My Friend

Beginning of the End

Heart bleeding
Hand held tight
On a wound
The night early
Full of anticipation
And empty with loss

How could this be?
Crazy
With troubled thoughts
And lost causes
I wait

Then it happened
A vibration
A sign!

"How are you? Did she get my gift? Good. Yes.
There's an old friend here that would like to
talk to you. Is that OK?"

My world transformed. "Yes."

"Hi." "Hi." "How are you..."

Inside I am crying like a baby
I love, therefore I am
The beginning of the end

Chapter Three:
Loss

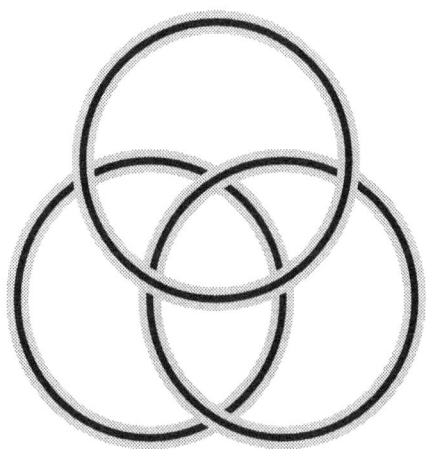

Ugly Tuesday

Phone call at work
My wife
Terror in her voice
Don't go
I'll hurry home

We arrive on the scene
Cold
Gray
Wet
Snow and ice, again

Who are these people?
Cameras
Lights
Uniforms and microphones
Do we wish to make a statement?!

We slog around
At the roadside
Waiting for an officer
Keeping our distance
Waiting for answers

A police car drives down
From the house
An officer emerges
There's been an altercation
One dead, one lives

Three shots
One to the chest
Two to the head, behind the ear
Mother is dead, father in custody
The children in despair

We grip our newborn son
In our despair and misery
And cling to God's mercy
To help us stand
On our feet

Love turned to tragedy
There are no answers
Our teachers and friends
Abandoned in our misery
Praying for our recovery

Ripped from the ground
Like a f*cking root
We cannot hide from the ugly truth

Crush of Deception

The truth speaks volumes

And crushes the deceivers

In my dreams

She Left Me

My baby she left me
I've been down so low
My baby she left me
I didn't even know

Been bangin' these drums
And poundin' these keys
Don't even know
When I'm down on my knees

There's a riot goin' on
Flowers in her hair
There's a riot goin' on
And she don't care

My baby she left me
She was never here
My baby she left me
Now I'm on the right

Save Me

One and one is two
Two and two is four
But what do friends need either for?

We need to love and we love to need
For this dependence we learn to grieve
To grieve because of loss of love
And despair for the reasons why

Why do we cling in short terms
To someone, something
Only to reject it in sweet disdain
When it no longer meets our worldly gains?

I think I know but it's hard to accept
It's because we are human, after all
And we need, we must, rock and roll

I love to rock and roll
I hate to crash and burn
Please forgive me for rock and roll
For love and hate
And save me from crashing
And burning

Into the Twilight

I don't want to be Sunday seconds,
I need to be Friday firsts.

What happened to us?
What can I do to wrong a right?

Where are you on this beautiful spring night?
I need you in my life and you're not here.

I'm starting to fade,
Into the twilight.

Give Me a Sign

I sit and watch the traffic flow
And wonder if I should go
Go into the great unknown
And lose myself
In the hope to find my way
In this crazy mad world
A world full of love and loss
And chaos

But I wonder if you will be there
And I fear that I will not find you

Please give me a sign
And I will go

Between Heaven and Hell

I am intoxicated
With heartfelt pain
And I do not know what to do

I can't move forward
And I can't backup
I'm stuck in a limbo without a clue

Somewhere between heaven and hell
The demons tease me
And the angels grieve

Alone I wait
And pray to God
That she will forgive me

Going Insane

I can't find myself
In this world of pain
I do not belong here
My case was not presented well
I need a new attorney
To lead me from this hell

This ink should be spilling out
A mountain of praise and thanks
For a wondrous life
But instead it is black and blue
A manifestation of each punch
I have received from you

A world of pain
Blinds my vision
And drives me insane

Waiting

It's unimaginable
That it's a crime
To speak your name
Or think of you
In these crazy times

When I think
Of the sane times
So close behind us
And the honest delivery
Of personal grief
And heart-felt convictions
Of remedies and plans
And dreams of tomorrows
We had

All gone now
Makes me sad
Tears form
My body trembles
And my soul weeps and waits...

Reconciliation

The dreams persist
And agonize
My loss is lost
Again and again

I need you
But you're free
And beautiful
In your freedom

In my dreams
I try to reconcile
Your freedom
And My Love

I Want to Call You

I want to call you
But I am afraid
Of your reaction
Do you think of me
And wonder too
Are you empty or full?

I want to call you
And share small talk
Of our days
Do you miss me
And feel a loss
Are you happy or sad?

I want to call you
And begin the recovery
Of our selves
Do you need me
And pray for help
From God above?

Disintegration

Convictions dismembered
Bonds broken and dissolved
As if they had never been
Nor will they ever be
Entropy is my enemy

Every night I create a vision
In a dream I assemble the pieces
And try to resolve the problems
That steal my health
And keep me crumbling in my self

Too many secrets bite my tongue
And bind my direction
A fool to transgression
Give me a light that I might see
A new path, a new destiny

In this strange crazy dark mad
That I find myself
Perhaps there is an option
A trail, a path, a new day
An unturned card, another way

Accusations

An ugly triangle of accusations
Born from domestic insecurity
Fed by need to help a friend
Helping hands to build a house of cards
For your love and our loss

The ugly face of domestic violence
Well known to us
We have looked upon it
And it has burned a hole in our hearts

A hole that cannot be fixed
With time or with space
How could we let it happen again?
True or false
Your strategy was good, My Friend

It was not hard
For us to believe
That he could drink and beat you
And make you need him
Your accusations, well placed

And it was not hard
For me to believe
That you were stroking your best friend's
husband
In my home
Your hand, well placed

And it was not hard
For your husband to believe
That I was the one
To hang your infidelity on
Your phone, well placed

You accuse him
I accuse you
He accuses me
A triangle of accusations
Started by you and ended by me

Backstabber

Once you were the second mother of my son,
A loving caring mother and friend,
A person that I could love and laugh with,
A respite from a stormy world.
A smile and a hug when I needed one.
I loved, My Friend.

Then you stabbed me in the back,
With knives forged from my words,
And sharpened with my tears.
FIRST in my home with your boyfriend,
SECOND in public by humiliation and insult,
THIRD by allowing our friends to think,
I was the problem,
When in fact, it was your own infidelity.

Was your strategy to let the messenger take
the fall?
Did you really think that the message would
not get through?
You're in deep shit now,
And you stink of it.

Where were you when I needed you?
A near fatal accident,
And I see you only once,
To deliver a fake hug,
And a card, not even from you.
So pitiful a delivery of concern,
You were pathetic.

Now you have your boyfriend to chase,
While his wife withers in pain,
And his children wonder why,
And your children wonder why,
And your husband takes another drink.

Does your boyfriend's manhood hold you in a
spell?
Does your womanhood pine for him?
Enough to lose so many loving friends?

It makes me sick to see,
After all, that you have no value.
I am ashamed of myself,
For my gross misjudgment,
And my waste of time,
On you.

You told my sister the truth,
About your second stabbing,
And you asked her never to tell.
Do you really think that my sister's love
Is weaker than your deceit?
How ridiculous!

Do you remember the first time we met?
You introduced yourself to me,
In my kitchen in my home,
With a handshake and a smile,
That cut me to the quick.
You worked your way into my home,
Into my life,

Into my family,
Without an invitation,
Assuming rights,
With no right at all.

I was the fool.
You played me for the fool,
To the end,
I thought we were best friends.

You told me the story once,
About your grandfather's rule,
To always give someone a second chance.
I've given you two,
Three strikes you're out.

As I pull your third and last knife from my
back,
I wonder why you can not simply tell the
truth,
And apologize,
And ask forgiveness,
But you will not.

You are consumed with yourself,
And care less about a friend.
Your consumption has blinded you,
You cannot see the results of your actions,
And poor decisions,
And now it is too late.

Count the friends that you have lost,
Count them, am I wrong?

With me you lost an entire family,
When you made your decisions,
You lost us all.

It makes me sick to the core,
That you betrayed your friends,
With lies and deceit.
You went on a man hunt,
Without a hunting permit,
And hunting out of season.
You could have done it right,
But you chose the wrong reasons.

Now I understand why,
When your boyfriend's wife,
(your friend!),
Kicked you out of her home,
Why you came back to us.
We were just another rest stop,
For your heavy insecurity,
Another place to hide,
From your dirty guilt and infidelity.

They say you can only truly hate,
Where you have truly loved,
I know this now to be true,
Backstabber, I hate you.

I am hurting so much that My Friend,
Would put three knives in me,
And make me bleed.

Your Face

If I could take it all back, I would
If I could tell a lie, I should
This pain that grips me, is real
This pain is not a lie

If you could have trusted me, to know
If you could have spared the lies, and betrayal
The friendship is over now, after all the years
Nothing left to do but wipe away the tears

The love turned to hate
The hate turned to pity
The pity, salt in my wounds
That may never heal

If I had known from the start
How this story would end
With your lies and my disgrace
I would have prayed to God,
Never to have seen your face

Before You

Sober thoughts of big troubled times
Leave me sitting here, looking for rhyme
Sorting out the truth from the lies
Reconstructing the events through your eyes

No matter how hard I try, I can't see
How you could be pushing and pulling at me
We broke it off and went separate ways
But you came crawling back, like it's OK

I wanna' get back to me
But I can't feel
How everything in my life
Will be the same
How everything in my life
Will be the same

BEFORE YOU!

Deal With It

Trouble will find you
There is no escape
We are all born
Into this prison of trouble

Only death will release you
From your sentence
Only trust in God
Will save you

Chapter Four:
Resolve

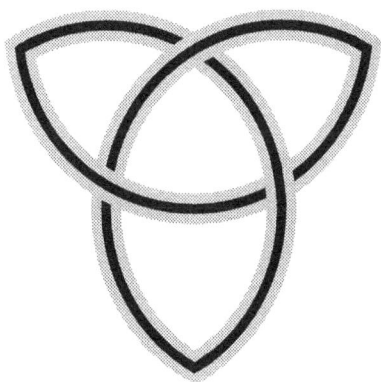

Survival

I believe that humans will survive the chaos of this world beyond any gene pool that has ever existed on this planet. Humans will accomplish this feat because of two fundamental differences between humans and all creatures of the Earth. The differences are:

1. we have Technology
2. we have Love.

Without Technology to adapt and change, we are beaten without the means to survive. Without Love in all of its forms and measures, we are broken without the will to survive.

The human brain cell and the human soul are aware that they exist and that they can be broken and they can be repaired.

Self-awareness of body and soul and the ability and resolve to mend them are our keys to survival.

Probation Begins

Sitting in the waiting room of the probation office of the district courthouse of our great state of our great country, I wait to meet my probation officer. Three months ago they peeled my car off a telephone pole while they slapped me in cuffs and hauled me in for DUI. Too many drinks, too little time, too powerful a car, too much anger, so close to home, and a serious error in judgment. Burned a red light, pissed off another driver, road aggression fueling my anger, pushing the limits of my troubled state, losing traction, hitting right curb, propelled over left curb (BOOM!), flipping on side with me in the air, sliding vertically, then smashing and crashing with huge force and thunderous BOOM!, the smell of tar and the taste of glass, the world changing to darkness and silence in a flash. In each death defying moment and motion, a picture is considered and stored, pictures that continue to haunt me. The car completely totaled and wrapped around the pole like some extreme masochistic sculpture of metal and wood. At the push of a single button, the seat belt, I dropped back to this Earth from my perch with only a scratch on my face and a bruise on my shoulder. Death kissed me that night and now she smiles and watches me as I begin a new journey with the angel of grace. Probation begins.

Counting the Days

This world will turn again
Into one more day
One more day that I can count
And measure my hate for you
One more day that I can wish you away

My world will clear again
Some sunny day
The clouds that rain down on me now
Will dry up and drift away
One more day that I can wish you away

Your world is crumbling
From your lies and deceit
The lies you've planted grow in this rain,
Creating the demons that will devour
Your soul and my pain

I'm just counting the days.

The Zounds of Love

The bleeding heart
Beats poetry
Pumping life
Through Cupid's wounds

The sound of love
Dripping
Heals in beautiful harmony
By God's wounds we mend

Vindication

My Friend, you have confessed!

And in my loss, I have won
And in my resolve, I will heal
I am free now to discover
The rest of my life

But you never would have admitted
Your guilt and transgressions
Of friendship and of love
Without me

By my crime and persistence for truth
By my witnesses and by your fear
You have crumbled and confessed
And I have won!

Nothing is sweeter
Than the moment of victory
Nothing is more bitter
Than irony in loss

My vindication on your path to salvation

Life is Good

Each step I take
On my ride on this ship
That spins and turns
Through the great void of space
Is a small step for me
And a large step for life

It's easy to look back
On the path that I have chosen
And consider the alternatives
Of trails not taken
Either overlooked or rejected
But the path is mine, my contribution
To the grand unification

It's difficult to look forward
And consider the infinite possibilities
But the future is mine
To make or to break
For better or for worse
Till death do us part

Like a marriage of chaos and free will
A beautiful marriage
That strengthens with time
Life marches on to fill the void
Leaving only footprints
Taking only pictures

Life is good!

My Love

You were 17,
Still a child,
And a woman,
When we met.

Our first date,
Set the pace,
For our lives:
Passion and virtue.

Our friendship,
Formed the fabric,
Of our love:
Respect and honesty.

Our marriage,
Created a bond,
An inseparable unity:
Integrity and tolerance.

Our son,
Was the proof,
Of God's love:
Divinity and grace.

My near death,
Shook me with fear,
Of our indifference:
Family and strength.

We've been together,
For 23 years,
I love them all:
I love you.

The road ahead,
Troubled I'm sure,
But always together,
We move on.

The Best is Yet to Come

A circle of resolution surrounds me now.

My wife,
My Love,
All that I do builds on her capacity for love
and forgiveness.

My sister,
My inspiration,
All that I think is filtered through her words
and inspire hope.

My brothers,
My strength,
All that I plan is strengthened by their
enthusiasm and trust in me.

My father,
My conscience,
All that I decide is weighed in his shoes.

My mother,
My first love,
Gives me strength and trust in family and
love.

My son,
My future,
Gives me hope that the best is yet to come.

50 Years

50 Years
Are half a century
And five times my son's ability
To be real
And seven years more than I am
In this world

50 years
Are more than most
In this world of six billion plus
Can hope to breathe
And awake in the morning
And weep or smile

50 years
Are yours
Treasure them and pray
For so many more
Happy anniversary Mom and Dad!

I am resolved to follow your lead.

The End

The end of friendship, of best times
The end of knowing, without a word
The end of smiles, laughter, hugs
Of short goodbyes

The end of plans, and hopes, and dreams
The end of just stopping by
The end of helping neighbor hands
When in need

The end of heartfelt friendship
It tears at my soul and burns my eyes
But now I'll stop, and say goodbye
Goodbye My Friend, I will miss you.

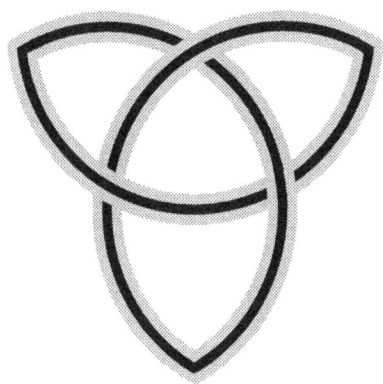

www.ingramcontent.com/pod-product-compliance
Lightning Source LLC
Chambersburg PA
CBHW080313030420

42337CB00011B/362